GARDEN ORNAMENTS
Pots, Pergolas, Pedestals, and More

Schiffer Publishing Ltd ®

4880 Lower Valley Road, Atglen, PA 19310 USA

E. Ashley Rooney

Cover: Courtesy of Seasons Four, Lexington, Massachusetts
Courtesy of The Field Gallery, West Tisbury, Massachusetts
Spine: Courtesy of Seasons Four, Lexingto, Massachusetts
Back cover: Courtesy of Seasons Four, Lexington, Massachusetts
Courtesy of The Preservation Society of Newport County
Courtesy of Elizabeth Schumacher's Garden Accents
Title page: Courtesy of Brass Baron Fountains and Statuary
Endsheets: Courtesy of D. Peter Lund

Library of Congress Cataloging-in-Publication Data

Rooney, Ashley.
Garden ornaments: pots, pergolas [sic], pedestals, and more/ by E. Ashley Rooney.
p. cm.
ISBN 0-7643-1956-6
1. Garden ornaments and furniture. I. Title.
SB473.5 .R63 2004
717--dc22
2003018726

Designed by Bonnie M. Hensley
Title page design by E. Ashley Rooney
Cover design by Bruce Waters
Type set in Bernhard Modern BT/Aldine 721

ISBN: 0-7643-1956-6
Printed in China

Published by Schiffer Publishing Ltd.
4880 Lower Valley Road
Atglen, PA 19310
Phone: (610) 593-1777; Fax: (610) 593-2002
E-mail: Info@schifferbooks.com
For the largest selection of fine reference books on this and related subjects, please visit our web site catalog at **www.schifferbooks.com**
We are always looking for people to write books on new and related subjects. If you have an idea for a book, please contact us at the above address.

This book may be purchased from the publisher.
Include $3.95 for shipping. Please try your bookstore first.
You may write for a free catalog.

In Europe, Schiffer books are distributed by
Bushwood Books
6 Marksbury Ave. Kew Gardens
Surrey TW9 4JF England
Phone: 44 (0)20 8392-8585; Fax: 44 (0)20 8392-9876
E-mail: Info@bushwoodbooks@co.uk
Free postage in the UK. Europe: air mail at cost.
Please try your bookstore first.

Contents

Courtesy of D. Peter Lund

Garden Ornament in the Landscape

Hugh J. Collins, Jr.

How does one integrate garden ornament within the landscape? Whether it is an antique statue, a sculptured fountain, or a whimsical piece of art, what is the best way to display it to its best advantage?

Garden ornament may often be an afterthought, a piece of art picked up while on vacation, something purchased on impulse, or a gift. One must begin the location process by deciding if the piece is to occupy a central spot as a focal point in the garden, or if it is to be placed as a subordinate element, discovered unexpectedly while interacting with the landscape.

Larger properties are generally designed as a series of outdoor "rooms," with some areas commanding more interest than others.

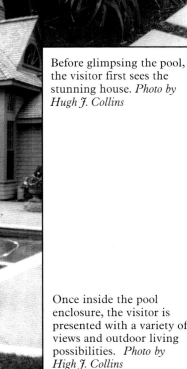

Before glimpsing the pool, the visitor first sees the stunning house. *Photo by Hugh J. Collins*

Once inside the pool enclosure, the visitor is presented with a variety of views and outdoor living possibilities. *Photo by High J. Collins*

A successful design alternately reveals and conceals, creating a sense of mystery as one is drawn forward through the landscape.

Garden ornaments can be placed at strategic spots in the garden or as a central dominant element. Creating an entire garden as a setting for displaying various pieces of art and ornament is another design approach. Nooks, grottos, and niche openings can be created and strategically placed so that each piece of ornament can be viewed to its best advantage. The garden becomes a joyful place to encounter, inviting one to move through and explore further. Specimen or unusual plants may also be used as focal points. A good example is "Harry Lauder's Walking Stick" (Contorted Filbert), which has a very striking and unique branch structure and overall appearance.

When designing the landscape surrounding your home, the best way to begin is to prepare a survey and analysis of the total property. Topography, mature trees, rock outcrops, views, and sun and wind orientation all play a role in the overall design scheme. A professional landscape designer will analyze and interpret this information and will prepare an existing conditions plan. This plan will illustrate both the opportunities and constraints of the site, and the design process can begin.

Landscape design typically starts with a schematic or conceptual plan delineating basic spaces and garden features. Client response and input become critical to the process at this time. The final design plan results from ongoing collaboration between client and designer. This involves many meetings and many "sketch plans" that explore a range of possible schemes, selection of materials, and design details.

The home owner's entertaining style, views, privacy, and sun and wind orientation are all important and need to be considered in the process of developing functional and successful outdoor living spaces. Garden ornamentation used as focal points or as subordinate elements will add interest and uniqueness to the home landscape.

The contours of this pool echo the shapes of the trees. *Photo by Hugh J. Collins*

When placed at random, garden ornaments may appear intrusive and arbitrary. Careful placement will help to achieve an integrated appearance so that artwork is visually connected with the surrounding landscape. Planting becomes the medium that ties garden ornaments with the rest of the landscape.

The challenge is to identify a unifying concept that "pulls everything together." Without a strong central idea, a landscape design can be a piecemeal assembly of plants, ornament, and construction elements that do not relate well to one another. A well-designed landscape plan is like fine art. It has a center of interest, unity, and balance.

Kinetic art may also be considered for added interest in the landscape. Large in-motion artwork that moves by force of wind or water can be placed as a focal point at the end of a long vista. A well-positioned mobile can add mystery and intrigue when viewed from a distance. When viewed at close range within passive "outdoor room" areas, the effect can be mesmerizing and even hypnotic.

Once the overall plan is completed, a landscape design professional will also coordinate the various trades required to install and complete the project. When the construction phase is managed by a landscape design professional, the homeowner benefits by dealing with a single individual, who schedules the work and maintains cost and quality control.

Garden ornament, be it statuary, artwork, or whimsical features, will add interest to a garden. The many illustrations in Ashley Rooney's book should serve as both a guide and a stimulus to creating a unique garden for yourself, your family, and your friends.

This pool provides a wonderful focus within the garden. *Photo by Hugh J. Collins*

Selecting the Perfect Garden Sculpture

Elizabeth Schumacher

A garden is the result of an arrangement of natural materials according to aesthetic laws; interwoven throughout are the artist's outlook on life, his past experiences, his affections, his attempts, his mistakes and his successes.
Roberto Burle Marx, Brazilian landscape architect

Figurative sculpture in the garden can be one of the best examples of the importance of a focal point. The sculpture can anchor a planting bed, lead the eye in a new direction, or provide a year-round accent visible from inside your home. So sculpture is important from a design perspective.

Even more importantly, sculpture is a wonderful opportunity to personalize your garden and reflect your particular interests. Figurative sculpture evokes an emotional response from the viewer and, because it is engaging, it will make your garden memorable.

A serene garden scene presided over by an antique bronze Buddha in Lee & Phoebe Driscoll's garden, Ambler, Pennsylvania. Photo by Dr. & Mrs. H. Ralph Schumacher

If you have an existing garden, first decide what you are trying to accomplish with the sculpture. Do you want to create an emotion or establish the feeling of a certain period? If you want to lighten the mood, consider a joyous lead figure like "La Brezza"—or The Breeze— with her arms outstretched to the sky. If your home is French Country, think about continuing the feel with Anduze pots or something that evokes the feel of France. A contemporary home may be the best place for a modern figurative or abstract bronze or a serene Japanese water basin or lantern.

I have seen effective garden use of all kinds of sculpture. Heroic figures of gods and warriors such as Diana, the huntress, suit some gardens. Other gardeners have commissioned bronze sculptures of children or grandchildren or have selected one of the many charming figures of children available. The adventuresome have placed a surprise such as a rhinoceros partially obscured by plantings.

A formal garden can be effectively accented by lead or cast stone figures of the four seasons or musicians along a wall or border. Pet lovers use sculpture of their animals near an entrance or at the edge of a planting bed. All of these emphasize the important contribution of sculpture — individualizing and personalizing your space.

One caveat. It is very important to think about scale when you choose a piece. With figurative pieces, the easiest way to handle this is to pick a life-sized piece. If you are not able to do this, you must create a setting that is in scale with the size of the piece you have chosen. To create this setting, you may use miniature or dwarf plants or, conversely, large plants with big leaves or bold forms. Scale is not an easy concept outdoors with no roof or walls and with living plants constantly changing.

Don't forget the purely practical aspects.

Cast stone will probably be the least expensive. Although this material is occasionally used by artists, most pieces are mass produced. The latter can still have artistic merit and can look great as they age but eventually the aggregate in the cement mixture will be exposed, which may impact the detail. Cast stone can vary widely in quality: dry cast statuary is the most expensive, and it resembles carved stone most closely. The beauty of cast stone is that it needs little or no maintenance

Hand-carved stone can be an original piece or can be a copy of an old traditional design or an earlier art work. Many hand-sculpted statues come from Vicenza, Italy. These are generally

A startling surprise sculpted by Simple in Mr. and Mrs. Harold Litvin's garden, Pottstown, Pennsylvania. *Photo by Dr. & Mrs. H. Ralph Schumacher*

This modern fountain by Harold Kimmelman centers the courtyard garden in Jude Plum's garden in Haverford, Pennsylvania. *Photo by Dr. & Mrs. H. Ralph Schumacher*

reproduction pieces from classical European gardens.

Italian sculptures are mainly limestone. This softer stone allows excellent detail and develops a wonderful antique patina fairly quickly but may need some protective silicone coating to keep it from absorbing moisture and breaking down during freeze thaw cycles. Some sculpture from Mexico or Bali can be even softer and will not hold up in northern winters. Vermont and other granite is so hard that it will last for centuries and consequently looks new in a garden for a very long time.

Lead is the classic material for English garden ornaments. This relatively soft material needs no maintenance and keeps its pleasant soft gray over the years.

Virtually all pieces are reproductions of known figures, and the parts of the sculptures are formed in molds. Because lead is so heavy, it can bend and break if it is not well supported. The workmanship quality can vary, which leads to different price ranges.

Lead was originally used as cheaper alternative to bronze. (Early lead planters were often actually made by estate plumbers.) Lead is still less expensive than bronze and can allow more delicate detail, which is important in figurative sculpture.

Antique iron sculpture, especially from France, can be wonderful but is very expensive. Antique iron is much more resistant to rust because the quality of iron was much better then than it is now. All iron needs some sort of protective coating, however, or it will eventually disintegrate. Because of the maintenance problems, little iron sculpture is done today.

Bronze is the Rolls Royce of garden materials. Most original art in the United States is now done in bronze using the lost wax method, which means that the artist works on the wax model of each casting. This labor-intensive process is expensive but results in true limited edition art that will appreciate in time.

There are also reproduction bronzes cast in Thailand, where there is a long history of making bronze Buddhas, say. These are not original pieces of art and are not limited edition but can still be delightful and long lasting. Bronze ages with an attractive green hue and can last with little maintenance for a long time. If you want to keep the original patina, then you will need to protect it with wax.

A new group of materials for garden sculpture are the resins and fiberglass. I have seen spectacular imitations of bronze, iron, lead, and stone in fiberglass. This material is lighter and easy to move and also extremely durable for outdoor use. Resins really require no maintenance.

Whatever the material for your sculpture, you must provide a stable base anchored below the frost line in your area. Without this, the ground can heave and topple even the heaviest of your carefully chosen pieces. Once seated firmly on a stable base, no matter what the season of the year, sculpture will enhance immeasurably your pleasure in your garden.

The purple chairs looking out at the purple flower beds complete this peaceful scene. *Photo by Dr. & Mrs. H. Ralph Schumacher*

Acknowledgments

Discovering garden ornaments is rather like embarking on a treasure hunt. There are so many beautiful ones: those that allow you to reach inside yourself and be in touch with the wind, the trees, and the land or those that tickle you or strike you with awe.

When I showed my father, author Stanley C. Schuler, the garden ornament photographs that my husband, Peter Lund, had taken, he shook his head in disbelief. He then admitted that he had thought I was crazy to write a book on this topic, but he hadn't realized how beautiful or how far-ranging garden ornamentation was–and my dad is really into gardens and art. Garden ornaments have come a long way.

Peter and I had a wonderful time seeking out ornaments on the market today. We visited gardens at landscape shows, shops, and private homes. We marveled at the creativity of today's garden artists.

One of my initial catalysts was the joy that Alan and Dorothy Lord of Brass Baron Fountains and Statuary take in their work. Subsequently, we met Elizabeth Schumacher of Garden Accents, with her uncanny knowledge of ornament and garden design. Their excitement about this field was contagious.

Over the Internet or through their work, I met many artists who had fascinating approaches to their work and who have participated in describing some of this art: Alice Calhoun, of Ace of Spades Garden Art, with her love of dancing, fairies, and magical gardens; Dave Caudill, a Kentucky sculptor of movable lyrical art, with his droll sense of humor; Tim de Christopher, a highly intuitive sculptor with a great grasp of reality and owner of New England Stoneworks; Peggy Ferguson, the co-owner of Pond Doc's Water Garden Center, with her enormous understanding of water gardens. Their insights enrich the book.

Through my earlier work, I had become entranced by the stunning work of Hugh J. Collins, Jr. I tracked down his firm and asked him to prepare the Foreword.

Peter Lund has been my good friend throughout this process. He, my father, and my sister, Cary Hull, have been listening, advising, and guiding me along the way.

Most of all, I acknowledge the garden ornaments themselves. Each is lovely, and there are many more where they came from. They frame the garden in their own ways, and each is a dream that has been transformed into reality.

Courtesy of Dave Caudill

Introduction

I have a garden; several of them, as a matter of fact. Hidden among the perennials stands my antique concrete pig, an antique armillary sphere towers above the hostas, and ivy cascades down the former wooden column from my front porch. On the terrace wall is my Centaur; in the herb pot is a sundial (a wedding present). A bench invites visitors to sit and watch the butterflies play in the sun. In the winter, I can see those ornaments from my windows. They decorate a barren landscape and remind me of summer. These objects bring a smile to my face. They set a tone, establish a style, and give me joy. Garden ornaments can do that .

The graceful statues, birdbaths, and pedestals that decorate lawns today are part of a long history of garden ornamentation that dates back hundreds of years. In the days of Rome, gardens were formal stage sets with sculpture set everywhere to show off the owner's taste or wealth. Under France's Louis XIV, royal architects lined symmetrical paths, terraces, stairs, and long reflecting pools with marble gods and goddesses. Servants clipped plants to form walls and arches or shaped them into emerald masonry.

In mid-eighteenth century England, Capability Brown and other great landscape architects created garden settings featuring dappled sunlight, natural groupings of trees and verdant woodland paths, punctuated with only a haughty stag or a ruined grotto.

In post-Civil War United States, Frederick Law Olmsted (1822-1903) was busily converting muddy regions of Boston, New York, and other major cities into tree-dotted, stylish areas. He and his minions preached a sophisticated simplicity in which only plants mattered and any artificial structures existed solely to display the plants.

The twentieth century, however, brought more suburbs, more lawns, and more lawn accessories. As al-

ways, Americans wanted to make their mark. Antique iron kettles, metal butterflies, and large rooster weather vanes joined chirruping fountains, frolicking pigs, and grimacing gargoyles. Garden art can range from a cast concrete snail to an original sculpture. The key is to select an accessory that suits your style. You might have the perfect nook for a beautiful statue that invites you to stop and enjoy the courtship of the cardinals whistling, "What cheer, what cheer." Or perhaps you want a burbling fountain.

Ornaments tell us where to look. They draw our eye, command attention, and emphasize the beauty of the garden. They pull us from lawn to dappled shade to the daylily bed. Some ornaments provide destinations; others call us to explore further. They can provide balance and texture, fill empty spots, and add color or sound to conceal something unsightly. Think of your yard as a picture frame. You want to engage the viewer through highlighting the landscape. The appropriate piece can serve as a visual oasis or a focal point.

This book presents over 400 garden ornaments, including human, animal, other world, and contemporary statuary; fountains; wall art and gates; urns and vases; moving sculpture; topiary; water gardens; and garden rooms. Many are described by their designer so you can visualize them through the designer's eyes and the camera. Others are described as they were observed.

There are many choices; whether it is an ornamental masterpiece or something you picked up at a garage sale, the right ornament in the right spot can make a startling difference to your garden.

Courtesy of Society for the Preservation of New England Antiquities.

Chapter 1

Human Sculpture

The classical female figure is a popular subject.
Courtesy of Seasons Four, Lexington, Massachusetts.
Photo by Siobhan Theriault

A garden sculpture need not be the work of famous artists like Henry Moore or Auguste Rodin. It doesn't matter whether it is made of marble, granite, bronze, lead, steel, or one of the many other materials. The only thing that counts is that it is a work of art—major or minor—capable of evoking an emotional response from the viewer—or at least the owner.

One statue of a callipygian woman provoked such laughter on my part that I had tears running down my cheeks. That, in turn, produced more laughter from those who accompanied me. Now when I look at the photograph of this sculpture, I recall that lovely summer day and the utter giddiness of finding something that provoked such laughter in someone as mature as I!

One of the nicer aspects of a garden sculpture is that it can beautify the winter garden. Like the poet Thomas Moore says, it can be the "last rose of summer left blooming alone." When you are designing a garden for summer and winter enjoyment, make sure that the sculpture will be prominent during the winter months. A garden ornament can appear quite different under a glaze of ice or against a bleak, brown landscape. It can be even more beautiful without the competition from the garden. Moreover, it ensures you that spring will come.

Garden ornaments can frame views, create vistas, and provide perspective. They point the way so your visitor can see the gorgeous stand of Asiatic lilies without noticing the fading alliums. They allow the viewer to relax on your terrace and still see the fine display of dahlias at the far end of the property. Ideally, your garden sculpture can stand silent among the flowers, signaling the beauties yet to come as the visitor walks through your garden, instead of you hustling your visitor around the garden saying, "See this and that." A sculpture defines the view without you acting as the talking guidebook and defeating the purpose of relaxing in the garden.

Many people today are deeply committed, even passionate, about creating beautiful gardens. The more harmonious elements (e.g., statuary, plants, and trees) contained in a garden, the greater the experiential pleasure. Some commission a statue; others scout out the right piece at flea markets or salvage yards; still other people haunt antique shops and garden design stores to find just the right statue that adds visual delight to their landscape.

As you can see from the pictures here, there is a wide range of sculptures to be obtained.

This contemporary female figure appears to be having much more fun than her classical counterpart. *Courtesy of The Field Gallery, West Tisbury, Massachusetts*

Is this female figure hiding from the ensuing tragedy? *Courtesy of Seasons Four, Lexington, Massachusetts. Photo by Siobhan Theriault*

The classical male always seems to be in charge. *Courtesy of Waterloo Gardens*

Unless he is piping in some temple. *Courtesy of Haddonstone 856 931 7011*

Another lovely woman. *Courtesy of Haddonstone 856 931 7011*

Emoting. *Courtesy of Seasons Four, Lexington, Massachusetts. Photo by Siobhan Theriault*

Or hiding among the roses. *Courtesy of Seasons Four, Lexington, Massachusetts. Photo by Siobhan Theriault*

This contemporary figure isn't hiding anything. *Courtesy of The Field Gallery, West Tisbury, Massachusetts*

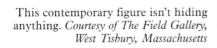

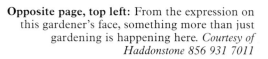

Opposite page, top left: From the expression on this gardener's face, something more than just gardening is happening here. *Courtesy of Haddonstone 856 931 7011*

Classical or contemporary, they look good. *Courtesy of Seasons Four, Lexington, Massachusetts. Photo by Siobhan Theriault*

Sitting among the flowers. *Courtesy of Equicraft*

Opposite page, bottom center: Sculptures can be dressed up for the season. *Courtesy of Seasons Four, Lexington, Massachusetts. Photo by Siobhan Theriault*

Opposite page, bottom right: They can be portrayed doing their shopping. *Courtesy of Seasons Four, Lexington, Massachusetts*

Another woman turns away.
Courtesy of Weston Nurseries of Hopkinton

Feeding the birds. *Courtesy of Magnolia Plantation*

They can mourn in a group. *Courtesy of Seasons Four, Lexington, Massachusetts. Photo by Siobhan Theriault*

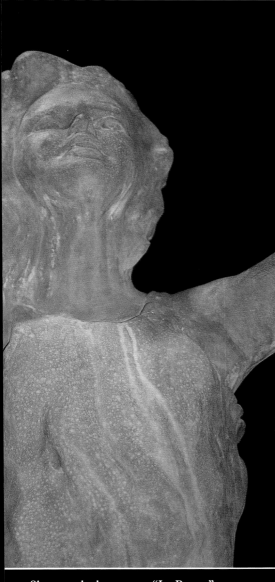

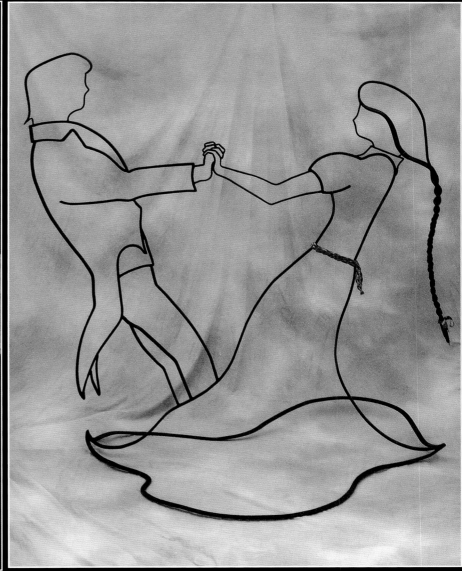

Shout to the heavens as "La Brezza"
does. *Courtesy of Elizabeth Schumacher's*

Dance with passion. *Courtesy of Equicraft*

Or jiggle on their pedestals. *Courtesy of The Field Gallery, West Tisbury, Massachusetts*

Sculptures of children tend to be cute. *Courtesy of Magnolia Plantation*

You see statues of adorable children. *Courtesy of Sfoggio Ltd.*

Children in the geraniums. *Courtesy of Seasons Four, Lexington, Massachusetts. Photo by Siobhan Theriault*

Thoughtful children. *Courtesy of Elizabeth Schumacher's Garden Accents*

Holding animals.
Courtesy of Magnolia Plantation

Playing with grapes.
Courtesy of Magnolia Plantation

Water. *Courtesy of Weston Nurseries of Hopkinton*

Or the flute. *Courtesy of Seasons Four, Lexington, Massachusetts. Photo by Siobhan Theriault*

Children can cast a shadow. *Courtesy of Elizabeth Schumacher's Garden Accents*

Children can bring joy. *Courtesy of Waterloo Gardens*

Serenity. *Courtesy of TJ's at the Sign of the Goose*

Curiosity. *Courtesy of TJ's at the Sign of the Goose*

25

St. Francis is a popular garden ornament. This one is made of lead by C. S. Paolo. *Courtesy of Florentine Craftsmen, Inc.*

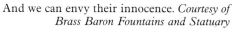

They can celebrate the joy of living as we see here in Girl on a Balance Beam by Elsa Martinus Chapman. *Courtesy of Elizabeth Schumacher's Garden Accents*

And we can envy their innocence. *Courtesy of Brass Baron Fountains and Statuary*

This St. Francis is actually meant to feed the birds.
Courtesy of Virginia Metalcrafters Brass Gallery

This rendition is more modern.
Courtesy of D. Peter Lund

You can get religious figures of all types.
Courtesy of Magnolia Plantation

Opposite page: Some of the modern ones are almost mesmerizing. This "Midway Garden Sprite" is a reproduction of the original by Frank Lloyd Wright.
Courtesy of Elizabeth Schumacher's Garden Accents

Let's not forget the angels. *Courtesy of Waterloo Gardens*

They come for all seasons. *Courtesy of Waterloo Gardens*

The Buddha symbolizes divine wisdom and good luck. *Courtesy of Castart Studios*

A Buddha rising. *Courtesy of Jackeroos*

Buddha/Quan Yin. *Courtesy of Stone Forest, Inc.*

Kuan Yin. *Courtesy of Castart Studios*

The Head of Shiva. *Courtesy of Castart Studios*

Life has its mysteries. *Courtesy of Elizabeth Schumacher's Garden Accents*

Such as this lone hand reaching out, hoping to touch some one. *Courtesy of Weston Nurseries of Hopkinton*

Chapter 2

Noah's Ark

Tim de Christopher

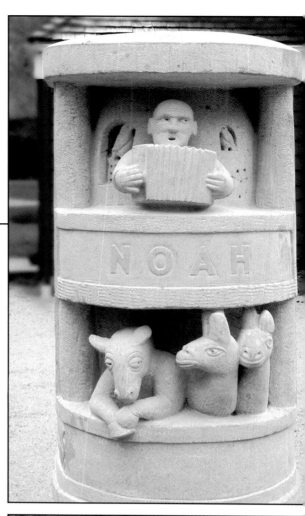

As the story goes, Noah was 600 years old when God suggested he build the fabled Ark.

From time in memoriam, from all ends of the earth, man has been telling stories of wit, wisdom, and wrath in the beastie world. From Cro-Magnon caves to the Hollywood hills, we imbue the world's creatures with our own great needs and deep longings, our fears, our fantasies, and our love. We ascribe to animals powers and abilities well beyond our own, and to ourselves (and each other) the varied attributes of every kind of creature, great and small, from the wormlike to the lionhearted. Whether creatures of the day or of the night, the animal world continues to serve as a limitless vehicle for our imagination.

As a sculptor, I prefer to work in a narrative vein. And when I work with animal imagery, I prefer giving them human attributes as a way to tell a story. The look in an eye, a tilt of the head, will speak volumes. We may not know the story, but we know there is a story, and so we are introduced to an element of tension.

Tension, a telling feature in all real and significant art, can extend to our gardens as well.

By tension, we do not necessarily mean anxiety. Tension can also be experienced as joy, excitement, curiosity, intrigue, or surprise for example—elements of balance and contrast punctuating a garden or a landscape. This kind of tension is well within the purview of a menagerie in our gardens.

I relish the idea of creating a miracle of some mad happiness, something utterly ridiculous that we cannot live without. Imagine an orchestra of pinstriped penguins about the lily pond, wooly stone sheep on a gentle slope, or elephants ambling in the cabbage patch.

On the other hand, we may long for a calming influence, a respite from our otherwise frenzied lives and worldly responsibilities. A solitary figure may be in order, a favorite creature, winged or otherwise; something calming, wondrous, steadfast, or wise, large or small or in-between.

Choosing is so much a matter of needs and desire. It is a process of self-discovery and self-expression, about trusting impulses and letting go. It is all in the manner of art, and art is always in the matter of life. Our choices, like our gardens, will always be in transition; just like life.

And the animals came two by two. *Courtesy of Tim de Christopher. Photo by Ariel Jones*

Love me, love my dog. *Courtesy of TJ's at the Sign of the Goose*

You might think twice about approaching this residence. *Courtesy of TJ's at the Sign of the Goose*

Opposite page, background: When many of us think of animals, we think of the dog, our faithful companion who waits for us with wagging tail. *Courtesy of Elizabeth Schumacher's Garden Accents*

Opposite page, right: This perky terrier probably doesn't know the meaning of patience. *Courtesy of Yardbirds*

This patriotic pair waits patiently for the parade. *Courtesy of D. Peter Lund*

Then there are the cat lovers. *Courtesy of Waterloo Gardens*

Many sculptors turn to the farmyard for inspiration. Here stands my pig in December. He gives me joy – no matter how deep the snow is. *Courtesy of D. Peter Lund*

Some houses in suburbia keep their cows on the front lawn. *Courtesy of D. Peter Lund*

You could have a grazing horse, instead. This one is only six feet high and nine feet long. *Courtesy of Richard S. Rothschild*

Many artists look to the prairies and forests for inspiration. Chris Williams makes a formidable, life-size "North American Bison." *Courtesy of Iron Works of Art*

Here stands his life-size, majestic moose in welded forged steel. *Courtesy of Iron Works of Art*

Should this elegant deer sit on your lawn? *Courtesy of Fleur*

This ferocious bear is not from a child's fairy tale. *Courtesy of Richard S. Rothschild*

J.P. Kennedy has some wonderful big cats.
Courtesy of John P. Kennedy

His tiger could be at your gates. *Courtesy of John P. Kennedy*

A lion is in the garden. *Courtesy of Haddonstone 856 931 7011*

Let us protect the elephants. *Courtesy of Savannah Hardscapes*

The Blind Man's Elephant. *Courtesy of Tim de Christopher. Photo by Ariel Jones*

Maybe in your garden "the wolf also shall dwell with the lamb, and the leopard shall lie down with the kid." *Courtesy of John P. Kennedy*

Have you read the poem about the six blind men and the elephant? This image is a detail of de Christopher's elephant. *Courtesy of Tim de Christopher. Photo by Ariel Jones*

Bottom left: Some hippos lurk in the greenery. *Courtesy of D. Peter Lund*

Bottom right: Others just look shy. *Courtesy of D. Peter Lund*

Giraffes can stand tall in your yard.
Courtesy of Iron Works of Art

You can even have a family of them. *Courtesy of Iron Works of Art*

Perhaps you prefer a more contemporary giraffe. *Courtesy of Yardbirds*

Let's not forget the monkeys. *Courtesy of John P. Kennedy*

Then we can look at the amphibians. This frog peers from the snowbank waiting for spring – something many New Englanders do. *Courtesy of D. Peter Lund*

In some gardens, frogs can leap remarkably high. *Courtesy of Weston Nurseries of Hopkinton*

Perhaps in your garden, "the time of the singing of birds is come, and the voice of the turtle is heard." *Courtesy of Willowbrook Garden*

You can have snails. *Courtesy of Fletcher Granite Co.*

And birds. A Trojan Chicken stands proudly. *Courtesy of Richard S. Rothschild*

This more traditional chicken might belong in a pot. *Courtesy of Sfoggio Ltd.*

A bird on the branch. *Courtesy of Richard S. Rothschild*

A "Stately Crane" made of rare tools and hardware stands sixty-seven inches high. *Courtesy of Iron Works of Art*

A pair of swans. *Courtesy of TJ's at the Sign of the Goose*

49

Rothschild's giant egret stands ten feet. *Courtesy of Richard S. Rothschild*

This bird stands about as tall. *Courtesy of Elizabeth Schumacher's Garden Accents*

Then there's the insect world. How about a dragonfly?
Courtesy of G. I. Designs

This green caterpillar could make a nice home in your garden. *Courtesy of Willowbrook Garden*

Ladybug, ladybug, fly away home. *Courtesy of Willowbrook Garden*

Chapter 3

The World Beyond

Statuary has often represented the mythical world. Ancient civilizations had nymphs protecting the springs, mountains, trees, seas and rivers; sphinxes guarding temples and asking riddles; satyrs dancing in woodland glens; women turning into swans. The list is immense.

By the beginning of the twentieth century, Egypt, China, and Japan also became important influences on garden design in the United States. The West Coast brought us Chinese foo dogs, Japanese cranes, and Asian temple figures. These elements also captivate us with their mystery.

As Alice Calhoun, a sculptor represented in this chapter, says, "The garden is a place of surprise and magical discovery and escape—a paradise on earth." She points out, "Our myths and archetypes have dark and light sides: dragons and ghosts, for example, vs. fairies and nymphs. Both enchant and intrigue us; both provide thrills; both provoke passionate responses. These kinds of figures can provide a sense of the pastoral, an escape from the mundane into a world where dreams of earthly beauty come true. They can also provide the chills and shock encountered as we move down the dark, twisty paths of our nightmares. They are the elements of the tradition of romance and the romantic, wild garden, as opposed to the parterres and urns of the formal, neoclassical garden.

Or we can have these haunting faces sculpted in lava by Bob Keegan. *Courtesy of Bob Keegan. Photo by Lois Keegan*

We can have happy faces peering from our garden. *Courtesy of Elizabeth Schumacher's Garden Accents*

These other worldly faces might send us down one road. *Courtesy of Bob Keegan. Photo by Lois Keegan*

Or another. *Courtesy of Bob Keegan. Photo by Lois Keegan*

A Balinese Dancer by Bo Atkinson can dance on your land. *Courtesy of Elizabeth Schumacher's Garden Accents*

You can have a dragon dwelling in your shrubbery. Depending on your imagination, the creature can be good or evil, intelligent or dumb, but always magical. *Courtesy of Equicraft.*

There are ugly dogs. *Courtesy of Savannah Hardscapes*

And threatening creatures. *Courtesy of A l'Ancienne Imports. Photo by © Linda Kane Parker*

Strange mythical beasts. *Courtesy of Elizabeth Schumacher's Garden Accents*

From legend, fable. *Courtesy of Weston Nurseries of Hopkinton*

And fairytale. *Courtesy of TJ's at the Sign of the Goose*

You can have elves that dwell in woodlands and enjoy a lifespan of centuries. *Courtesy of Elizabeth Schumacher's Garden Accents*

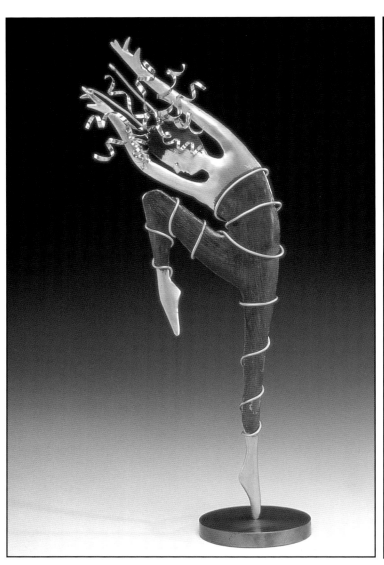

This firefly fairy will dance through the day and night in your garden. *Courtesy of Ace of Spades Garden Art. Photo by David Egan*

This demure water spirit would love to live near a fountain or pool in your garden or even on a wall in your bath. *Courtesy of Ace of Spades Garden Art. Photo by David Egan*

Alice Calhoun's sparkling fairies stand approximately twenty-eight inches. She calls this one "Joy." *Courtesy of Ace of Spades Garden Art. Photo by David Egan*

Let's not forget those beautiful but terrifying gargoyles. From Gothic and horrific to human and funny, gargoyles can be delightful. *Courtesy of D. Peter Lund*

Courtesy of D. Peter Lund

Courtesy of D. Peter Lund

Courtesy of D. Peter Lund

60

Chapter 4

Contemporary Sculpture

Whatever sculpture is used, it should complement the surrounding features, not detract. Some might say that abstract ornaments might be more fitting in the garden of a contemporary home; others believe that each ornament makes a statement about you and your style. It's your choice.

A manhole is removed, and *voila*, there's a sculpture. *Courtesy of Seasons Four, Lexington, Massachusetts. Photo by Siobhan Theriault*

One luscious pear makes a wonderful, terra cotta accessory. *Courtesy of Sfoggio Ltd.*

Allison Armour-Wilson's contemporary sculptures use modern materials in all-embracing, geometric shapes. The "Third Eye" has a huge presence. *Courtesy of Allison Armour-Wilson*

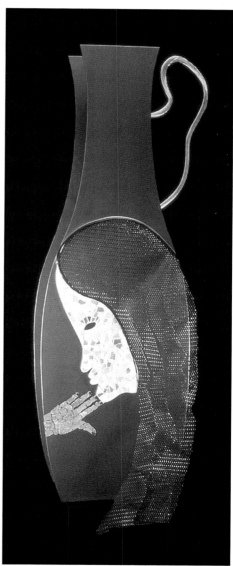

This object is known as "Spiritman Calling." *Courtesy of Vassa - SpiritMetal*

This odd looking bird hangs messages. *Courtesy of Fine Garden Art*

While the Doves of Peace by Robert Winship swoop toward the sky. *Courtesy of Elizabeth Schumacher's Garden Accents*

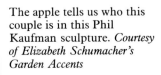

The apple tells us who this couple is in this Phil Kaufman sculpture. *Courtesy of Elizabeth Schumacher's Garden Accents*

Stone lanterns were first used in ancient Shinto shrines, where they served as votive lights. In the sixteenth century, Japanese tea masters included stone lanterns in Buddhist tea gardens to light the way. *Courtesy of Stone Forest, Inc.*

This stainless steel trellis is an elegant framework for flowering vines. *Courtesy of Dave Caudill*

This image shows details of a stainless steel "starfish" sculpture supporting a mandevilla.
Courtesy of Dave Caudill

The entire starfish is portrayed here.
Courtesy of Dave Caudill

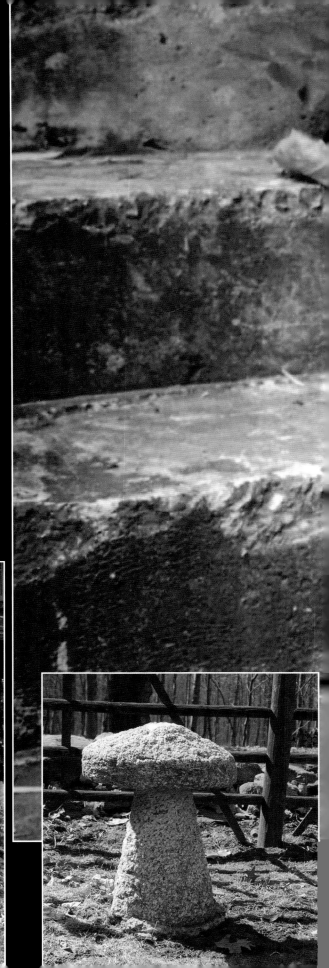

The pineapple symbolizes hospitality. Here, as a weathered stone finial, it is also an object of beauty. *Courtesy of Fleur*

Opposite page, bottom right: Staddle stones were used for many centuries as supports for granaries and corncribs. In the twentieth century, they became garden ornaments. *Courtesy of Fleur*

Want to play chess? Checkmate.
Courtesy of Castart Studios

These terra cotta chimney lanterns also became ornaments. *Courtesy of A l'Ancienne Imports.*
Photo © Linda Kane Parker

This sculpture is composed of triangular stainless steel pieces polished to mirror brightness. They slot together and sit on another piece of polished steel to maximize the reflections that occur as you wander around it. *Courtesy of Allison Armour-Wilson*

Chapter 5

Sundials, Gazing Balls, Pedestals, and Obelisks

Today, sundials are popular garden ornaments, linking different parts of the garden or acting as a focal point. But they are not just decoration; they are an ancient method of telling time.

The oldest known sundials date back to 1500 BC, when the Egyptians invented them to help calibrate their 365-day calendar. Subsequently, the Greeks introduced them to the Romans, who are said to have been the first to use sundials in their gardens. There they marked the passage of time and asked the passerby to consider how he or she spent his life with such choice mottoes as "Time flies" or "Death conquers all."

In ancient Greece and Egypt, sundials supplied the only form of accurate timekeeping. Public places often had large sundials to signal the official hours of the business day. As civilization grew, people used sundials to reset their clocks and watches, which were frequently inaccurate.

Today, sundials vary from a simple vertical dial to an elaborate armillary and can be cast in lead, bronze, iron, or carved from stone. They can be placed on a pedestal or level with the ground. Colorful flowers or a formal herb bed complement them. Whatever. As my neighbor says, "They are charming."

A sundial watches over my flower garden.
Courtesy of D. Peter Lund

An ornate sundial suits some. *Courtesy of TJ's at the Sign of the Goose*

A beautiful copper sundial marks the hours.
Courtesy of TJ's at the Sign of the Goose

This man carries the weight of the world.
Courtesy of TJ's at the Sign of the Goose

Sundials can focus on favorite hobbies or pursuits. *Courtesy of Waterloo Gardens*

This sundial is perfect for the water lover or bird lover in your life. *Courtesy of Outdoor Décor*

While others like more modern sundials. *Courtesy of TJ's at the Sign of the Goose*

Sundials
even look
great in the
winter.
*Courtesy of
D. Peter
Lund*

Victorian gazing balls have been known for over 400 years. These silvered shimmering spheres, available in kaleidoscopic hues, can capture an entire garden in their spheres.

Gazing balls have been called Spheres of Light, Gazing Globes, Rose Balls, Good Luck Balls, Victorian Balls, Witch Balls, and Globes of Happiness. They have been used to symbolize wedded bliss; to repel evil spirits, ill fortune, and illness; and to wish for good luck. According to some, enterprising Victorian women placed gazing balls so they could see if visitors were approaching or if they needed more lemonade!

Gazing balls have become more interesting these days. *Courtesy of Roy Gohmann*

They have assumed new colors and stands. *Courtesy of Roy Gohmann*

Many gardeners enjoy using architectural fragments in their gardens. Columns, pedestals, plinths, brick piers, or concrete blocks can be used to raise a flower-filled pot or gargoyle to some prominence in the garden.

This row of columns suggests the impressive ruins of a classical colonnade. *Courtesy of Elizabeth Schumacher's Garden Accents*

Columns can be useful or decorative, classical or contemporary. *Courtesy of Savannah Hardscapes*

This column can bring the garden into sharper focus because it catches the viewer's eye. *Courtesy of Elizabeth Schumacher's Garden Accents*

This beautiful bust depicts a young Roman maiden. The renowned XIX century sculptor Charles Francis Fuller sculpted the original. *Courtesy of Haddonstone 856 931 7011*

Opposite page: This pedestal is unique. *Courtesy of Weston Nurseries of Hopkinton*

These sleek, wrought iron designs fit any décor. *Courtesy of Achla Designs*

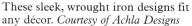

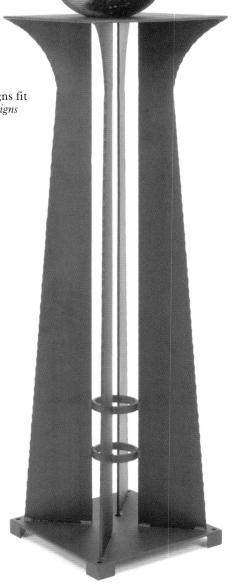

The original of this impressive Equine Head was excavated at Civitavecchia near Rome and later acquired by the Medici family who sent it to Florence. *Courtesy of Haddonstone 856 931 7011*

This pedestal would make a statement wherever it is placed. *Courtesy of Achla Designs*

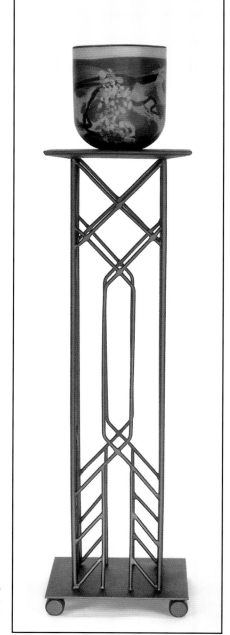

Obelisks are slim, four-sided tapering monuments that draw the eye. Created from a single great piece of stone, they usually terminate in a pointed or pyramidal top. Their solidity, permanence, and verticality attract the onlooker to explore further.

Ancient Egyptians dedicated obelisks to the sun god and generally placed them in pairs before the temples, one on either side of the portal. In most cases, deeply incised hieroglyphs and drawings ran down the four sides.

Ancient Roman gardens often featured obelisks, where they could function as sundials. Ultimately, obelisks became part of the eighteenth century garden.

This obelisk can be used to great effect at the end of a long vista, in a courtyard, or formal garden area. *Courtesy of Haddonstone 856 931 7011*

Obelisks can be very impressive – even in a small garden. *Courtesy of Seasons Four, Lexington, Massachusetts. Photo by Siobhan Theriault*

This dazzling, contemporary obelisk reflects the sunlight and the garden. *Courtesy of Allison Armour-Wilson*

Here, a stone fragment juts from the lawn, acting as a perch for the bird. *Courtesy of The Field Gallery, West Tisbury, Massachusetts*

This contemporary design could be considered an obelisk or a bird perch. *Courtesy of Tom Torrens Sculpture Design, Inc.*

Some ornaments play double duty. They may be decorative, but they also have a job to do. They may conceal ugly hoses or pipes, edge flowerbeds, cap faucets, or support vegetables or flowers. *Courtesy of GI Designs*

A trellis can support your plants and provide a vertical accent in your garden. *Courtesy of Willowbrook Garden*

Other objects can also act as obelisks, catching your eye, defining a corner. Certainly, stones can be used to signal attention. *Courtesy of D. Peter Lund*

In the early twentieth century, the wellhead became popular in American gardens. The wellhead was a block of stone that had been hollowed out to contain the well. Water was introduced from a spring or pipe. Today, there are few visible wells, but there are some ugly pipes around. Here, we have an artificial wellhead that conceals those ugly pipes. *Courtesy of Weston Nurseries of Hopkinton*

Chapter 6

Wall Art

Wall art is another way of embellishing our gardens. An appropriate plaque can enrich our surroundings, bring the mysteries of the heavens down to earth, make us laugh on a cold gray day.

A large ornament such as a trellis can even screen the mundane or the ugly. Wall art and plant life can complement and accentuate each other.

This mural creates movement and direction and perhaps some erotic thoughts. *Courtesy of The Field Gallery, West Tisbury, Massachusetts*

Wall hangings can be mythical such as this Centaur, who hangs on my wall. He is thought to represents wisdom and old age. *Courtesy of D. Peter Lund*

Subjects of wall plaques can range from terrifying. *Courtesy of Waterloo Gardens*

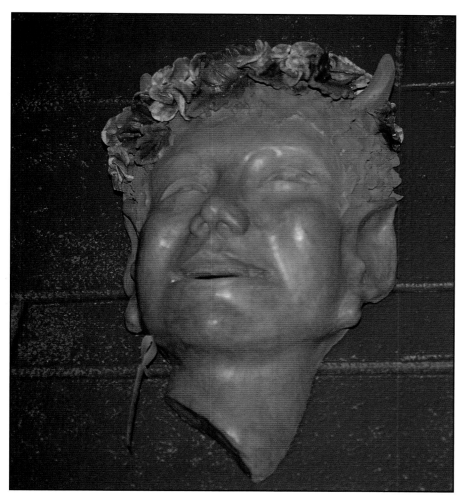

To lighthearted as in this terra cotta head of Bacchus by Betty Reeves. *Courtesy of Elizabeth Schumacher's Garden Accents*

So often, garden art displays women looking beautiful. *Courtesy of Savannah Hardscapes*

Karen Lipeika uses Repousee, an ancient art form, to make her sculptures. Soft metal is her "clay." *Courtesy of Karen Lipeika*

And men at work. *Courtesy of Haddonstone 856 931 7011*

There are plaques of cherubs. *Courtesy of Savannah Hardscapes*

And musical scenes as in this Gladding McBean, architectural terra cotta wall plaque. *Courtesy of Elizabeth Schumacher's Garden Accents*

Wall art has many subjects. Here, it features birds. *Courtesy of Karen Lipeika*

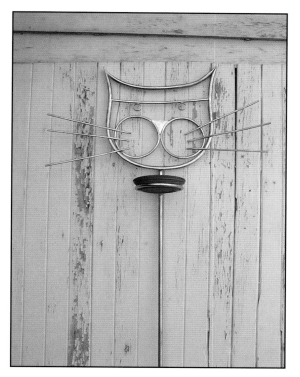

Here we have cats. *Courtesy of GI Designs*

Horses. *Courtesy of Karen Lipeika*

Wall art can also be contemporary in feeling.
Courtesy of Karen Lipeika

Spiritual. *Courtesy of Castart*

Then there are the forces of nature. *Courtesy of Castart*

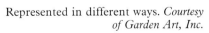

Represented in different ways. *Courtesy of Garden Art, Inc.*

Of course, there are the gargoyles. *Courtesy of Elizabeth Schumacher's Garden Accents*

Often the mundane is turned into wall art. This bell was made in the early 1900s. *Courtesy of D. Peter Lund*

This trellis is another way of decorating a bare wall or concealing an ugly area. *Courtesy of GI Designs*

Think of this against your garage
or in front of your compost bin.
Courtesy of GI Designs

This beautiful screen is a wind and
traffic buffer. *Courtesy of D. Peter Lund*

Gates act as doors to the garden; they are an opening through a wall, fence, or hedge, but they can also be an augury of what is to come.

Ideally, an entry gate extends a welcome to guests without surrendering a sense of security. It should blend with the style, design, and size of its home or garden and tolerate frequent use. Here, a gate acts as a lovely decoration and signals the homeowner's interest or occupation. *Courtesy of Achla Designs*

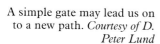

A simple gate may lead us on to a new path. *Courtesy of D. Peter Lund*

Opposite page: At the beginning of the twentieth century, wrought iron gates and fences symbolized good taste and a certain class. Often imposing, they can make a strong initial impression on visitors about the gardener and the garden they are to meet. This beautiful gate is certainly designed for grand entries. *Courtesy of D. Peter Lund*

Chapter 7

Jardinieres, Urns, Troughs—or Just Plain Pots

Pots allow you to grow your garden on a porch, rooftop, or in your driveway — wherever you wish. You can place a pot to direct the eye of the onlooker to a new vista, to nudge the viewer further on the path, or to solve an architectural problem. Pots are functional as well as ornamental.

Pots go back to the beginnings of civilization. The ancient Egyptians used pots – we know that from hieroglyphs. Asian civilizations used pots. When archeologists excavated Pompeii and Herculaneum, they found perfectly preserved clay olive oil jars among the ruins. During the Renaissance in Italy, wealthy landowners used stone urns and vases. By the late nineteenth century, gardening in containers was a standard practice.

Although many attractive containers are manufactured and sold specifically for use with plants, great containers come from many sources. Some like bronze, glass, hollowed out rocks; others like old wheelbarrows, chimney flue pipes, and claw-footed bathtubs. Many like to coordinate the pot with the design of the space.

Pots embellish a garden, provide emphasis, and accent — whether the garden is large or small. *Courtesy of D. Peter Lund*

This Regency Gothic, octagonal jardiniere has double-quatrefoil panels with alternate acanthus and rose relief bosses. *Courtesy of Haddonstone 856 931 7011*

This urn guards a path in the gracious Magnolia Plantation gardens in South Carolina. *Courtesy of Magnolia Plantation*

Lunaform's pots are known for their seductive, graceful lines. *Courtesy of Lunaform*

Lunaform pieces are handturned on wheels, in concrete, and completely steel-reinforced. *Courtesy of Lunaform*

This pot was found at the end of a northeastern garden. *Courtesy of Seasons Four, Lexington, Massachusetts. Photo by Siobhan Theriault*

Britain's National Trust commissioned Haddonstone to make this replica to replace damaged vases at Cliveden, Buckinghamshire. *Courtesy of Haddonstone 856 931 7011*

This vase is an antique reproduction from Portugal. *Courtesy of Casafina*

The surprising combination of basket-weave and dragon's feet is characteristic of the XIX century naturalistic style of ornament. *Courtesy of Haddonstone 856 931 7011*

Opposite page: This handsome bowl acts as a planter for impatiens. *Courtesy of Weston Nurseries of Hopkinton*

Some like the basket of fruit. *Courtesy of Seasons Four, Lexington, Massachusetts*

This handsome Baroque-style container has fish-scale and reed decoration. The interior base is removable to allow shrub roots to reach underlying soil. *Courtesy of Haddonstone 856 931 7011*

Others keep their pot empty. *Courtesy of Fleur*

Still others like a more modern look. *Courtesy of Nohra Juille. Photo by D. Peter Lund*

This intricately laced urn makes a statement. *Courtesy of D. Peter Lund*

This elevated pedestal planter is in the style of a similar arrangement in the Royal Summer Palace Gardens, Bangkok. *Courtesy of Haddonstone 856 931 7011*

This bowl reaches for the sun. *Courtesy of Lunaform*

A lotus basin can be a planter or a fountain. *Courtesy of Elizabeth Schumacher's Garden Accents*

A water jar becomes a lovely garden urn. *Courtesy of Jackeroos*

An ancient urn.
Courtesy of Fleur

Half a face. *Courtesy of Waterloo Gardens*

Half a brain. *Courtesy of Savannah Hardscapes*

An alpine planter. *Courtesy of Stone Forest, Inc.*

Pot your plants individually and then make your window box. *Courtesy of GI Designs*

Chapter 8

Moving Sculpture

Motion acts as a magnet. The bird's flight, the fountain's jet of water, the butterfly's graceful meander—all invite our attention and reward it with a spontaneous rush!

Moving sculpture breathes life into its setting, whether a country estate or a cabin in the woods. Abstract silhouettes, fanciful images, and balanced forms bring discoveries with each new view. When change becomes part of the picture, art dances in an evolving choreography with plantings, wind, and sky. Moods and meanings are reborn season after season.

Dave Caudill, one of the sculptors represented in this chapter, says, "My own garden is an eclectic universe, reflecting my passions, curiosities, and whims, which are bound to change, right? And aren't gardens all about reframing anyway? The abundance of masses, textures, and colors changing throughout the year; it's nature giving us a parade to live in! Having art that changes within the garden is just getting with the program!"

Picasso once said, "It takes many years to become childlike." The spirit of play can take a lot of forms but may be most at home in the garden. Moving art offers us special opportunities to rekindle that spirit as it reflects light and introduces new rhythms, sounds, and shapes.

As Caudill says, "Viewing art sparks creativity in all of us! When I come home preoccupied and rediscover a little piece of joy, that sudden shift opens the door to new ideas."

Dave Caudill's "Still Dancing" is a stainless steel sculpture, seven feet tall.
Courtesy of Dave Caudill

Caudill says, "...you know, my sculptures are just big toys! When I turn them over and see them upside down, I always get new ideas. And placing them in different areas means different light conditions with new plant combinations too." *Courtesy of Dave Caudill*

This "Memory of a Garden Breeze" is launched from a small garden bed to bring the sky to the garden. *Courtesy of Dave Caudill*

This second picture illustrates how the character of a kinetic sculpture changes.
Courtesy of Dave Caudill

And changes... *Courtesy of Dave Caudill*

…And changes. "Gardens make me smile - at least some art ought to do the same!" *Courtesy of Dave Caudill*

Allison Armour-Wilson, the sculptor, says, "These ever-changing, mirror-polished tubes are my personal favorite. They glint as they revolve around, going orange in the sunset and looking particularly amazing in the snow and frost." *Courtesy of Allison Armour-Wilson*

Modern materials in sweeping geometric shapes can enhance conservative as well as modern gardens. *Courtesy of Allison Armour-Wilson*

Opposite page; Top: The garden may be sleeping, but this ornament brings heightened texture to it. *Courtesy of Dave Caudill*

Bottom: Like nature itself, the sculpture is transformed by the weather. *Courtesy of Dave Caudill*

The designs of Tom Torrens can be found in gardens and settings all over the world. This is a standing bird feeder. *Courtesy of Tom Torrens Sculpture Design, Inc.*

Gongs are particularly useful in a large garden. *Courtesy of Tom Torrens Sculpture Design, Inc.*

They reverberate with sound, calling the distant gardener, heralding the visitor. *Courtesy of Weston Nurseries of Hopkinton*

Even a weathervane is a moving sculpture. We found this marvelous pig in Maine. *Courtesy of TJ's at the Sign of the Goose*

Trains fascinate many of us. About a century ago, English railroad enthusiasts began building miniature railroad systems in their gardens. In the 1960s, the first, weatherproof garden locomotives were introduced; in the 1980s, engines modeled after historic American trains were developed.

Garden railroads create new worlds in your backyard. Suddenly, you have mountains, lakes, and vast forests. You have old mills and bustling towns, bridges and tunnels. You can create your own private kingdom.

Courtesy of Weston Nurseries of Hopkinton

Courtesy of Weston Nurseries of Hopkinton

Courtesy of Weston Nurseries of Hopkinton

Courtesy of Weston Nurseries of Hopkinton

Courtesy of Weston Nurseries of Hopkinton

Courtesy of Weston Nurseries of Hopkinton

Courtesy of Weston Nurseries of Hopkinton

Courtesy of Weston Nurseries of Hopkinton

All aboard. *Courtesy of Weston Nurseries of Hopkinton*

Chapter 9

Living Sculpture or Topiary

Sculptures of living shrubbery and trees is an ancient art form dating back to the Egyptians and Romans. Examples can be seen today at Disneyland, the Epcot Center, and the Orangerie at Versailles.

Pliny the Elder, who lived from 23 to 79 AD, traced the invention of topiary to a friend of Julius Caesar during the first century BC. When Rome fell, so did topiary—not to be revived until medieval times when fruit trees were trained flat or espaliered against inner castle walls.

During the Italian Renaissance, verdant peacocks, bears, globes, and ships adorned the nobility's gardens. Later, the Dutch began clipping trees and bushes into whimsical birds and beasts in their carefully trimmed gardens. With the reign of the Dutch-born William of Orange and Mary, topiary reached new heights in England in the seventeenth century. Whimsical shapes spread over the English landscape, while the French preferred a

Green Animals Topiary Garden, owned and maintained by The Preservation Society of Newport County, Rhode Island, has one of the oldest topiary gardens in the nation. *Courtesy of The Preservation Society of Newport County. Photo by D. Peter Lund*

Its gardens have more than 80 sculptured trees and shrubs in the shape of geometric forms and animals such as lions, tigers, and teddy bears. *Courtesy of The Preservation Society of Newport County. Photo by D. Peter Lund*

highly manicured look with rows of geometric figures and flat topiary designs in a knot garden style.

In the United States, topiary started in Williamsburg, Virginia, around 1690 with geometric forms dotting gardens. With their characteristic ingenuity, American gardeners dressed up their gardens with a wide repertoire of forms. They used topiary to accentuate the layout of formal estate gardens, to provide a focus for informal plantings, and to add an element of surprise.

In 1984, New York City's Rockefeller Center startled tourists and inhabitants alike with its wild topiary animals wandering between the skyscrapers. Today, topiary is practiced by gardeners who enjoy being on the cutting edge.

The animals resemble velvet creatures in their privet coats. Shaping a plant into a topiary sculpture is not for those who seek immediate fulfillment. It takes time to coax a vine to cover an arbor or to carve boxwood into a fanciful Alice in Wonderland shape. *Courtesy of The Preservation Society of Newport County. Photo by D. Peter Lund*

A fourteen-foot sailfish or "Sail out of the Water" by Joe Kyte hovers over the pond. Constructed in 1996 to replace a lightning-struck Medjool date palm, this fish is still going strong with monthly trimming. *Courtesy of Joe Kyte*

Joe Kyte's swan fountains make an unusual pool adornment. *Courtesy of Joe Kyte*

Opposite page: Some of the animals have inhabited the garden since 1912. The gardeners at Green Animals Topiary Garden pinch, trim, and clip every week to create their three-dimensional topiary zoo. When the giraffe lost its head in a hurricane, the gardener made a new head after shortening the neck. *Courtesy of The Preservation Society of Newport County. Photo by D. Peter Lund*

His gator with friends is sixteen-feet long.
Courtesy of Joe Kyte

What a triumphal elephant!
Courtesy of Joe Kyte

What small child wouldn't be delighted to have this dinosaur roaming their land? *Courtesy of Green Piece Wire Art*

Spring green frogs, docile ponies, fluffy rabbits, and proud roosters. Animals have always lifted our spirits and brought joy to our lives. Anyone can have a full menagerie in his or her back yard. *Courtesy of Green Piece Wire Art*

Green Piece's stork is a lovely addition to any water garden. *Courtesy of Green Piece Wire Art*

This image illustrates the use of a frame to grow topiary For low maintenance topiary, place your form over a plant rooted in the ground. Let the plant (e.g., ivy) grow into the form. *Courtesy of Green Piece Wire Art*

Topiary Joe makes full-size human forms. *Courtesy of Topiary Joe*

The golfer resting on his laurels
resides along the "19th hole."
Courtesy of Topiary Joe

Chapter 10

Fountains

Water has the rare capacity to introduce an aura of tranquillity into your garden. Whether in the form of a formal or naturalistic pool or as a simple stream and waterfall, water attracts us.

Moving water is perhaps the most fascinating. Maybe it is the sound of water spraying the air or perhaps it is the way it cascades back down, moving water has a mesmerizing effect.

Creating a beautiful fountain for your home is not that complicated. Preformed units are widely available and easy to install. Most of your work is done with them. Many striking fountains come as a complete kit with a fountain jet already included. If you installed a suitable power supply when building the pool, you should be able to wire in the fountain and have it running within a day.

Or you may want to investigate a liner-constructed waterfall.

The original for this exquisite triple fountain stood in the Cloister Court of Eton College, Windsor, England. The Haddonstone replica has ornate pedestals supporting three, decorative shell bowls surmounted by a naturalistic bud. The water cascades from tier to tier, creating a symphony of water sounds. *Courtesy of Haddonstone 856 931 7011*

Opposite page: Imagine the coolness of several fountains, the pleasant trickling of water blocking ambient sound and enhancing a feeling of peacefulness. *Courtesy of Seasons Four, Lexington, Massachusetts. Photo by Siobhan Theriault*

In this unusual waterfall, we see the garden through the water and reflected in the water, and the sunshine sparkles all around. The clear sphere is full of water, which emerges through a hole at the top and then cascades down around the sides. The sphere sits on a mirror-polished stainless platform with the integral pump hidden underneath. The entire piece sits in a stainless steel dish; it can be made any size. *Courtesy of Allison Armour-Wilson*

In this image, this versatile, self-circulating fountain features simple leaf moldings to the bowl, complementing the design of the support. Here, it has a "Boy with Dolphin" centerpiece. *Courtesy of Haddonstone 856 931 7011*

This thirty-nine-inch high, Mizubachi fountain elicits a response similar to viewing ocean waves or sitting beside a mountain stream. *Courtesy of Stone Forest, Inc.*

The music of the Lotus Bowl calls to listeners. Here, it is combined with three dolphins as its centerpiece. *Courtesy of Haddonstone 856 931 7011*

129

The water springs to the graceful statue. *Courtesy of D. Peter Lund*

The fountain among the roses. *Courtesy of Seasons Four, Lexington, Massachusetts. Photo by Siobhan Theriault*

This forty-five inch tall Anthurium Fountain is a melodious addition to any yard. *Courtesy of Ray Gohmann*

The Diamond Fountain is a hand-carved granite sculpture, which combines the simplicity of Japanese style with contemporary design. *Courtesy of Stone Forest, Inc.*

Imagine the coolness of this green nook and the grand Acanthus Lead Fountain (over seven feet high) on a hot summer day. *Courtesy of Florentine Craftsmen, Inc.*

Traditionally used in Gothic architecture to throw rainwater from the walls of a building, this Haddonstone design is specifically intended to act as a wall fountain. *Courtesy of Haddonstone 856 931 7011*

Today, you can find (with some searching) gutter mouths in the shapes of various animals. *Courtesy of D. Peter Lund*

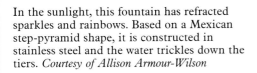

In the sunlight, this fountain has refracted sparkles and rainbows. Based on a Mexican step-pyramid shape, it is constructed in stainless steel and the water trickles down the tiers. *Courtesy of Allison Armour-Wilson*

The Cattail and Iris Fountain is constructed from copper resting on a stone base. It is thirty to thirty-four inches tall. *Courtesy of Ray Gohmann*

Your garden pool will probably be the only one in the neighborhood with its own
hippo fountain. *Courtesy of Brass Baron Fountains and Statuary*

Or perhaps you prefer an alligator. *Courtesy of Brass Baron Fountains and Statuary*

Some may prefer a more delicate fountain such as this Cattail Fountain with its graceful arches of water. *Courtesy of Ray Gohmann*

Wild Flower, an elfin young girl with a lily hat, is a reproduction of an exquisite bronze by sculptor Edward Berge. She models the cherubic pose that was popular with garden artists in the 1920s. *Courtesy of Brass Baron Fountains and Statuary*

Alternating shell tiers create a unique look on this variation of the classic tier fountain. *Courtesy of Ray Gohmann*

Ducks have delighted children and artists with their sleek beauty and vibrant colors for generations. *Courtesy of Brass Baron Fountains and Statuary*

Fountains don't have to be big to make a splash. This twelve-inch-tall Waterlily Fountain is copper on stone. *Courtesy of Ray Gohmann*

The Sky Mirror Fountain keeps water moving over the granite, creating a soothing, contemplative atmosphere. *Courtesy of Stone Forest, Inc.*

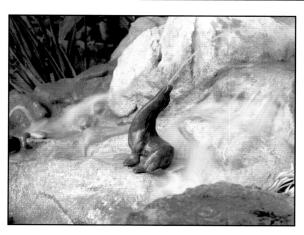

A great seal makes spraying water fun. *Courtesy of Brass Baron Fountains and Statuary*

Many different ornaments are available for use in and around the pool: from simple spouting seals and charming children to multi-tiered lotus bowls. *Courtesy of Brass Baron Fountains and Statuary*

Others might like a contemporary design such as these stainless steel balls on a copper wall fountain. *Courtesy of Ray Gohmann*

Opposite page: Some might prefer a welcoming pineapple. *Courtesy of Waterloo Gardens*

There is a lot of diversity in fountain ornaments – not only in quality and price. *Courtesy of D. Peter Lund*

But also in design. This limited edition bronze is by British sculptor David Goode. *Courtesy of Elizabeth Schumacher's Garden Accents*

Chapter 11

Pools, Ponds, and Birdbaths

Peggy Ferguson

The Barton pond was one of the favorites featured in Pond Doc's Tour de Ponds. This inviting waterfall leads visitors through the entrance arbor and down flagstone stairs to the lush gardens below. *Courtesy of Peggy Ferguson*

Pools, ponds, and birdbaths stimulate more of our senses than any other element in the garden. A gentle stream provides us with a wonderful spot for peaceful meditation while offering birds a place to play and bathe. Waterfalls play relaxing music, and we can watch water splash-dance against the rocks as it finds its way to the pool below. A night-blooming water lily fills the evening with wonderful fragrance. Fish, frogs, and dragonflies provide endless hours of entertainment as they frolic about the pond.

The addition of water to the garden can be as simple as placing a birdbath or fountain in the middle of a perennial bed. You can transform an old jug into an object d'art by adding a pump and a piece of hose or you can have a sophisticated water feature such as a large koi pond. Either way, the water element becomes a focal point. Only our imaginations limit us.

The possibilities are endless. From formal raised fountains to natural streambeds, it's all a matter of personal taste. Reflecting pools are peaceful. Waterfalls are lively. Frog and fishponds are educational.

Many do-it-yourself projects are just waiting to be born. People enjoy the satisfaction of installing a pond themselves, which is not a hard thing to do. With the help of experts, research, and the right equipment, a novice gardener can install a low-maintenance pond that stays crystal clear and healthy. Although swimming pools generally require the expertise of qualified contractors, handy homeowners build state-of-the-art ponds everyday with help and advice from pond professionals.

The recipe for transforming an ordinary garden into a music-filled center of activity and entertainment for the whole family is an easy one. Just add water.

This water garden is lush despite the heat of summer. *Courtesy of D. Peter Lund*

If you watch carefully, you can almost see the water lilies closing at the end of the day. *Courtesy of D. Peter Lund*

You can create your own waterfall by utilizing the way water moves over and around the stones. As the water flows, it reflects light and produces sound. *Courtesy of Weston Nurseries of Hopkinton*

By letting the water flow over a waterfall and into a pool, you can create a water feature on your property. Once you plant around it, you frame the picture. *Courtesy of Weston Nurseries of Hopkinton*

A pavilion provides an intimate nook on a big pond. *Courtesy of Achla Designs*

The use of accessories, such as decorative potted plants and whimsical characters in and around a pond, offers glimpses of the owner's personality. *Courtesy of Peggy Ferguson*

Some water gardens have elegant statues such as this mermaid. *Courtesy of Brass Baron Fountains and Statuary*

Or this boy riding a sea horse. *Courtesy of Brass Baron Fountains and Statuary*

Or statues on an island. *Courtesy of Magnolia Plantation*

Most of us don't think of anything this elaborate. *Courtesy of Haddonstone 856 931 7011*

Generally, we visualize something simpler. *Courtesy of D. Peter Lund*

Wall fountains are another way to add the flow of water to a garden. *Courtesy of Seasons Four, Lexington, Massachusetts. Photo by Siobhan Theriault*

149

This antique marble water wall made with Lapis Lazuli is from India. *Courtesy of Elizabeth Schumacher's Garden Accents*

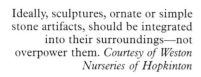

Ideally, sculptures, ornate or simple stone artifacts, should be integrated into their surroundings—not overpower them. *Courtesy of Weston Nurseries of Hopkinton*

This rustic garden pool seems part of its environment. *Courtesy of Seasons Four, Lexington, Massachusetts. Photo by Siobhan Theriault*

The rough birdbath adds drama to the garden pool. *Courtesy of Stone Forest, Inc.*

A copper birdbath perches on the edge of the stream. *Courtesy of Stone Forest, Inc.*

This classic birdbath stands in the roses.
Courtesy of D. Peter Lund

Chapter 12

Garden Rooms, Ruins, and Birdhouses

For many years, gardeners have been bringing the outdoors inside, but what about the reverse — bringing the indoors outside!

A stone wall here, a meandering pathway, a hedge there, perhaps a nook and a cranny, and you can have a house surrounded by garden rooms. Some rooms might surround us with the flowers and perfumes of a garden. Others might focus on a flowing fountain or a playhouse.

Some decorators alter the original elements in the garden to create their own vision.
Courtesy of Nohra Yuille. Photo by D. Peter Lund

The garden is revealed only as we pass through it. The transitions between areas or rooms enhance the romance of the whole. Every area has a focal point; this area is the moss room. *Courtesy of Nohra Yuille. Photo by D. Peter Lund*

This garden is all about special small areas, places removed from our everyday experience. Here, we have a dining area surrounded by rock walls. The lightly separated spaces within this area contribute to a sense of expansion. *Courtesy of Nohra Yuille. Photo by D. Peter Lund*

The "light" of the candle is a shell. *Courtesy of Nohra Yuille. Photo by D. Peter Lund*

The stone floor sets off the green of the chairs. *Courtesy of Nohra Yuille. Photo by D. Peter Lund*

Little things such as this decorative accessory and the old millstone make a difference. *Courtesy of Nohra Yuille. Photo by D. Peter Lund*

The transitions between the garden rooms enhance the magical feeling. Here, we leave the dining area through these rounded steps curving out of the wall. *Courtesy of Nohra Yuille. Photo by D. Peter Lund*

Codman House, c. 1740, in Lincoln, Massachusetts, was a gentleman's country seat. *Courtesy of Society for the Preservation of New England Antiquities. Codman House, Lincoln, Massachusetts. Photo by D. Peter Lund*

The grounds feature perennial beds and a reflecting pool filled with waterlilies. *Courtesy of Society for the Preservation of New England Antiquities. Codman House, Lincoln, Massachusetts. Photo by D. Peter Lund*

There is a hidden Italianate garden, c. 1900. *Courtesy of Society for the Preservation of New England Antiquities. Codman House, Lincoln, Massachusetts. Photo by D. Peter Lund*

Classic stauary has a significant place here. *Courtesy of Society for the Preservation of New England Antiquities. Codman House, Lincoln, Massachusetts. Photo by D. Peter Lund*

For those of us, who cannot design our own garden room, there are all sorts of possibilities out there – such as this lovely pergola. *Courtesy of Haddonstone 856 931 7011*

Or perhaps you want a pavilion. *Courtesy of Achla Designs*

Which can be found in various styles. *Courtesy of Charleston Gardens®*

There's a modern tree design.
Courtesy of GI Designs

And a classic design. *Courtesy of Seasons Four, Lexington, Massachusetts. Photo by Siobhan Theriault*

Another possibility is something known as a ruin. *Courtesy of Haddonstone 856 931 7011*

Think of finding this in a quiet garden nook...
Courtesy of Haddonstone 856 931 7011

...or this c.1850 iron and stone well. *Courtesy of Fleur*

Arbors like gates and obelisks can point to a New World in the garden. We see them ahead of us as we stroll through a garden. They draw our attention and pull us along. They establish a new style to be found just beyond.

Gates, doors, and arbors not only separate areas, but they can bring them together. *Courtesy of GI Designs*

Arbors also can change focus or direction. *Courtesy of GI Designs*

Outdoor furnishings can provide a feeling of graciousness and hospitality. *Courtesy of Charleston Gardens®*

A faux-bois bench sits upon the lush grass, inviting you to sit and enjoy your surroundings. *Courtesy of Fleur*

There are many different types of benches. They range from traditional wood to marble reproductions to contemporary slabs. Many of them could stand alone as garden ornaments. *Courtesy of Weston Nurseries of Hopkinton*

A garden should have a bench for you to enjoy the view, listen to the bubbling fountain, or smell the flowers. *Courtesy of Weston Nurseries of Hopkinton*

When you sit on a bench, proposals are given; promises made; stories are told. *Courtesy of D. Peter Lund*

Gardening can be for the birds. *Courtesy of D. Peter Lund*

167

Imagine the sight of brilliant gold finches, red cardinals, azure blue jays and orange orioles in your backyard. Picture them eating, bathing, singing, and raising their young all within a few feet on the other side of your windows or on the edge of your patio. It can happen.

This Victorian Cottage birdhouse is the quintessential wren house. *Courtesy of Outdoor Décor*

The Contemporary Beach house attracts many birds. *Courtesy of Outdoor Décor*

If you can provide the right types of food and shelter, in the right places, you will have maximum numbers and varieties of birds to enjoy every day of your life. *TJ's at The Sign of the Goose*

Many birds
would be
happy here.
*Courtesy of D.
Peter Lund*

Resources and Suppliers

Aces of Spades Garden Art: dance, English gardens and ancient forests, folktales, and comparative mythology inspire Alice Calhoun's magical sculptures. Her joyful, copper garden sculpture includes dancing fairies, elves, wood nymphs, and magic animals. Most pieces are created in either the traditional green verdigris or a new purple patina. She has received awards of excellence, been in traveling exhibitions, and featured in various magazines. 112 East First St., Hermann, Missouri 65041 Tel. (573) 486-3060.
www.alicecalhoun.com
alice@gardendance.com

Achla Designs' functional yet beautiful products are based on the owner's enjoyment of gardening and profession as an architect. Skilled craftsmen in Poland make the firm's heirloom-quality, wrought iron products, which are powder-coated for rust protection, and individually hand forged and welded. 65 Arbor Way, Fitchburg, Massachusetts 01420 Tel. (800) 626-1114.
www.achla.com
info@achla.com

A l'Ancienne Imports feature antique (c. 1500-1900) architectural elements and accessories from the Burgundy region of France. The items in its showroom constantly change as the firm receives new shipments. Glen Ellen, California Tel. (707) 996-2550.
www.alaimports.com

Alice Calhoun: See Aces of Spades Garden Art.

Allison Armour-Wilson's collection of sleek modern sculptures, water features, and garden accessories uses modern materials to enhance traditional as well as contemporary gardens. She works primarily in mirror-polished stainless steel and clear acrylic so her pieces reflect their surrounding spaces in new and exciting ways. Her work has been featured regularly on BBC and ITV television and in many publications. Baldhorns Park, Rusper, West Sussex, England RH12 4QU Tel. 01293 871575.
allison@netcomuk.co.uk

Brass Baron Fountains and Statuary specializes in the design and production of brass fountains and sculptures that create excitement and elegance in indoor and outdoor settings. Cast by skilled artisans, many of these handcrafted sculptures are replicas of European masters. Pieces created by Brass Baron convey feelings of sentiment, magic, and amusement and delight a discriminating clientele who appreciate quality craftsmanship. 10151 Pacific Mesa Blvd., San Diego, California 92121 Tel. (800) 536-0987.
www.brassbaron.com

Casafina offers an old stone collection imported primarily from Portugal. Its lawn and garden accessories are cement antique reproductions. 301 Fields Lane, Brewster, New York 10509 Tel. (845) 277-5700.
office@casafinagifts.com

Castart Studios, founded in 1993, produces original design sculptures, birdbaths, water features, planters, and wall art for home and garden decoration. Many of their designs are based on the history of art. Suitable for indoor or outdoor use, their products are made from proprietary blends of concrete and have weather-resistant finishes. 2145 Keating X Rd., Saanichton, B.C., Canada V8M 2A5 Tel. (250)652-3397 Tel. (1-888)316-4464.
www.castartstudios.com

Dave Caudill is a Kentucky sculptor who makes unique trellises and movable, lyrical sculptures of stainless steel. Using slender rods, he builds linear artworks that also support vining flowers and vegetables. His more massive, abstract sculptures can be rolled into different positions to change their contributions to a landscape. 1261 Willow Ave., Louisville, Kentucky 40204 Tel. (502) 454-4769.
dave@caudillart.com

Charleston Gardens® is a mail order and Internet commerce company dedicated to providing quality furnishings and accessories for the garden and home. It seeks to provide a unique collection of merchandise that complements the beauty found in nature and reflects the beauty of the gardens and architecture found in its namesake city. 61 Queen St., Charleston, South Carolina 29401 Tel. (843) 723-0252.
www. charlestongardens.com

Hugh J. Collins, Jr., Landscape Designer, Inc., offers clients a truly comprehensive design/build program, overseeing projects from beginning to end. The firm specializes in residential landscapes of distinction for discerning clients. Typical projects include swimming pools, tennis courts, site grading and drainage, driveway and parking layout, stone masonry, irrigation, lighting, and planting plans. The firm's dedicated team has provided satisfaction to more than 500 customers over the past 25 years. 225 Main St., Wenham, Massachusetts 01984 Tel. (978) 468-1942.

Village West 1045 Main St., Osterville, Massachusetts 02655 Tel. (508)420-8715.

www.hjcollinsdesign.com
hjcollins.design@verizon.net

Tim de Christopher, the owner of New England Stoneworks, has been creating original work for public and private settings for over 20 years. His work ranges from small, highly personal sculpture to large-scale, site-specific installations, architectural stonework, and restoration projects. He has worked extensively at the Cathedral of St. John the Divine in New York City and is currently developing a monumental installation entitled The Cathedral Project. 9 Butler Place, Northampton, Massachusetts 01060 Tel. (413) 586-7496

www.ohmysoul.org
tim@ohmysoul.org

Equicraft owner William Kuegel enjoys working with all types of metal. He began his metalsmithing career shoeing horses after graduating from the University of New Hampshire. In 1977, he and his wife, Lynn, first used horseshoe nails to create a line of unique hand-made ornaments. They also create life-size garden sculptures, created from steel with accessories of copper, pewter, and brass. 36 Earle Drive, Lee, New Hampshire 03824 Tel. (603) 659-7919.

www.equicraft.com
info@equicraft.com

Peggy Ferguson: See Pond Doc.

The Field Gallery's joyful sculpted figures are designed for frolicking in a garden. Tom Maley's sculpture can be found dancing in the garden of the gallery. His sculpture is available cast in bronze or in urethane resin with a white marine paint finish. Both mediums are weather-hardy. State Road, P.O. Box 664, West Tisbury, Massachusetts 02575 Tel. (508) 693-5595.

fieldgallery@adelphia.net

Fine Garden Art specializes in one-of-a-kind art objects for the garden. The artist, Jill Nooney, collects scraps of metal, often old farm equipment, and reconfigures them as sculpture, frequently whimsical in nature. Her works have been featured in *Fine Gar-dening Magazine, USA Today, People. Places and Plants,* and the TV show "Chronicle." Bedrock Farm, 45 High Rd. Lee, New Hampshire 03824. Tel. (603) 659-2993.

www.finegarden.com
Jill@finegarden.com

Fletcher Granite Co., LLC, is a single source supplier of granite for architectural, civil, and landscape projects. It has quarry deposits that have supplied stone for over a century, a tradition of hand craftsmanship, and the technical expertise necessary to assist design professionals. 275 Groton Rd., North Chelmsford, Massachusetts 01863.

www.fletchergranite.com
info@fletchergranite.com

Fleur specializes in garden ornaments and antiquary. Most ornaments are found in France and England, often in the countryside and from estates. Pieces range from cast iron urns to stone finials, statuary, and planters. Fleur carries a wide assortment of French Faux Bois pieces. 84 Lexington Ave., Mt. Kisco, New York 10549 Tel. (866) 397-3300.

www.fleur-newyork.com

Florentine Craftsmen, Inc., a family business in New York for over 80 years, manufactures high quality garden ornaments, statuary, fountains, furniture, and planters from lead, bronze, aluminum, iron, and stone. Motifs range from the elegant to the whimsical, many in the classical European tradition. 46-24 28th St., Long Island City, New York 11101 Tel. (718) 937-7632 .

www.florentinecraftsmen
Florentine@mindspring.com

Garden Accents was inspired by Elizabeth Schumacher's appreciation for the importance of ornaments in good garden design and her world-wide search for quality pieces for her own award-winning garden. Founded in 1979, Garden Accents offers original art, antiques, and contemporary ornaments from the USA, Europe, Africa, and Asia. Voted "Best of Philly," Garden Accents has an inventory of over 3,000 pieces and will also help design and install custom and commissioned work. 4 Union Hill Rd., West Conshohocken, Pennsylvania 19428 Tel. (610) 825-5525 or (800) 296-5525.

www.gardenaccents.co
askLiz@garden-accent.com

Garden Art, Inc., imports raw castings from Mexico, which it hand finishes in its Connecticut facility. Products are made of sand cast aluminum, a low maintenance product for the home and garden. Cast aluminum is weighty enough that high wind is not a concern yet not so heavy that objects are immovable. It is as durable as iron but does not overheat in the sun. 598 Deming Rd., Berlin, Connecticut 06037 Tel. (860)

829-0707.
www.garden-art-inc.com

GI Designs are seen in *Garden Design*, *Homestyle*, *Southern Living*, and *National Gardening* magazines and have appeared at *Sunset Magazine's* 2001 Idea House and at the Denver Botanic Gardens. Its collection of attractive, affordable, copper and brass creations makes the perfect addition to your home or garden. The firm offers a wide range of distinctive trellises, arbors, weathervanes, cupolas, and custom design work. 700 Colorado Blvd., #120, Denver, Colorado 80206 Tel. (866) 287-8660.
www.GIDesigns.net
cs@gidesigns.net

Ray Gohmann is a native of New Albany, Indiana. He has been working in copper as a sculptural medium full time after setting aside his landscaping tools in 1998. His sculptural works and fountains illustrate an affinity for water and natural forms and instinctive dislike of straight lines. His handmade, original designs are generally one of a kind. 2818 Silver Creek Drive, New Albany, Indiana 47150 Tel. (812) 944-3226.
gohmann@thepoint.net

Green Animals Topiary Gardens of the Preservation Society of Newport County began in 1880. Boxwood-lined ornamental gardens surround eighty pieces of topiary, including a lion, a dinosaur and a giraffe, sculpted in privet, yew, and boxwood. Green Animals is one of America's oldest topiary gardens. The estate is also home to a variety of other historic gardens and a Victorian summer residence that is open for tours. The Preservation Society of Newport County Society's collection of antique toys is housed on the second floor. Cory Lane, Portsmouth, Rhode Island Tel. (401) 847-1000.
www.newportmansions.org

Green Piece Wire Art, Topiary, and Garden Sculpture, as seen on HGTV Canada (2002) and HGTV USA (2003), invites you to experiment, shape, create, decorate, and enjoy its hand-crafted, three-dimensional sculptures. Each topiary piece is made of closely woven wire and fabricated to scale, imitating nature. Customers can quickly create classical or whimsical figures by planting these sphagnum moss-filled frames. P.O. Box 260, Bridge Station, Niagara Falls, New York Tel. (905) 679-6066 or (1-877) 956 5901.
www.greenpiecewireart.com
info@greenpiecewireart.com

Haddonstone, established in 1971 to produce high-quality decorative stonework, is now one of the leading manufacturers of ornamental and architectural stonework. Its collection has grown to over 500 designs, with every item being the work of highly skilled craftsmen. The construction and renovation of palaces, stately homes, National Trust properties, international hotels, state buildings, and gardens, as well as private houses and gardens of every description have employed its pieces. Haddonstone (USA) Ltd., 201 Heller Place, New Jersey 08031 Tel. (856) 931-7011.
www.haddonstone.com
Haddonstone Ltd., The Forge House, East Haddon, Northhampton NN68 DB U. K. Tel. 0160 477 0711.
www.haddonstone.co.uk

Iron Works of Art: see Chris Williams.

Jackeroos are Australian cowboys, and the Jackeroos company got its start in 1984 by offering authentic Australian outback gear. Today, the company imports a wide variety of items, most of which are made in Fiji or the Outer Islands of Indonesia, including Bali and Lombok. The traditional "Sasak" pottery from Lombok is made entirely by hand and fired with wood. 428 Route One, Edgecomb, Maine 04556 Tel. (207) 563-7900 or (800) 443-7970.
www.jackeroos.com
jack.kennedy@jackeroos.com

Keegan's mystical, often haunting faces resemble those in the European Alps, etched into the craggy cliffs by the forces of nature. Keegan, who studied under master carvers in Austria and is the author of well over 10,000 such faces in nineteen countries, now creates them in lava rock. This medium makes his artwork suitable for year-round outdoor placement. 927 Mt Eyre, Newtown, Pennsylvania 18940 Tel. (800) 543-8330.
www.Alpine-Art.com
TheKEEG@aol.com

John P. Kennedy creates lions and tigers and bears... and that's just the beginning! These concrete sculptures are not just life-size, but life-like in stance and color. He has been enamored with animals since the age of five when his father brought him home the *Golden Nature Guidebook –Mammals*. Today, the firm custom makes stone carvings or terra. 8844 No. 5 Road East, Delphi Falls, New York 13051 Tel. (315) 662-7242.
jkenned1@twcny.rr.com

Karen Lipeika uses Repousee, an ancient art form, to make her lovely sculptures. Soft metal is her "clay." Once she has established the overall shape, she begins refining the detail. She enjoys the rhythm of pounding the hammer into metal, the freedom to shape, reshape, and bend the material, first on one side then the other. Ultimately, she brings the shape into a new form.
www.sculpt-it3d.com
sprngr@netscape.net

Lunaform makes garden planters and urns, a number of them replicas of vessels found in ancient Greek and Roman gardens as well as the classic gardens of America. All pieces are hand turned on wheels, in concrete, and completely steel reinforced. They are available in a wide variety of natural color and textural finishes. Lunaform LLC., P.O. Box 189, West Sullivan, Maine 04664 Tel. (207)422-0923.

www.lunaform.com

Magnolia Plantation, which is listed in the National Register of Historic Places, has, for over three centuries, been the ancestral home of the Drayton family. Today, it is considered to have "the most beautiful garden in the world" and the oldest, major public garden in the United States. Magnolia Plantation is the centerpiece of Ashley River history and played important roles in the early days of settlement, the Revolutionary War, and the Civil War. 3550 Ashley River Rd., Charleston, South Carolina 29414 Tel. (843) 571-1266 or (800) 367-3517.

tours@magnoliaplantation.com

OutdoorDecor.com/The Arthur Wilbur Company, Inc., is a leading Internet retailer of unique home, garden and outdoor decorative merchandise such as sundials, weathervanes, birdfeeders, mailboxes, and door ornamentation. 3740-F Resource Drive, Tuscaloosa, Alabama 35401 Tel. (800) 422-1525.

sales@outdoordecor.com

Pond Doc's Water Garden Center's Peggy Ferguson, the co-owner, is the editor of "What's Up, Doc" and the Webmaster of www.ponddoc.com, which was chosen as one of *KoiCarp Magazine's* top-10 sites for koi health. The Water Garden Center is a full-service supply center that specializes in helping do-it-yourselfers create state-of-the-art, low-maintenance ponds and is one of a limited number of facilities in the United States where koi and goldfish can be taken for health diagnosis. 762 N. Main St, Alpharette, Georgia 30004 Tel. (770) 663-6325.

www.ponddoc.com
peggy@ponddoc.com

Richard S. Rothschild says if an animal "is not flying, running, or creeping, there at least should be tension in just standing still, as if the animal had been in motion a moment before and in another instant will be again." His work often incorporates weathered barn siding and split rails and vividly colored stains. When his life-size sculptures are not outdoors in gardens, fields, or around pools, they can be found in houses, lobbies, or atriums. 175 Knibloe Hill Rd., Sharon, Connecticut 06069 Tel. (860) 364-1915.

www.rothschildsculpture.com

richroth@discovernet.net

Savannah Hardscapes imports many custom architectural items, including planters, urns, statues, fountains, and garden furniture from sources in England, France, Greece, Italy, and Spain. Its collection focuses on high quality pieces that will distinguish gardens or interiors. Its stone yard location offers three acres of natural stone, cobblestones, antique tiles, and statuary. 513 West Jones St., Savannah, Georgia 31401 Tel. (912) 443-9000.

www.savannahhardscapes.com

Seasons Four, Lexington, Massachusetts, has something for the estate garden to the weekend plot. It offers decorative accessories, perennials, and plants. It has ornamental stock like evergreens, topiary, and Japanese trees and tropical plants, including hibiscus, orchids, begonias, Australian trees, and palms. During the winter, it carries a fair amount of stock so you can find something green any time of year. 1265 Massachusetts Ave Lexington, Massachusetts 02420 Tel. (781) 861-1200.

Sfoggio, Ltd. offers Italian Majolica for the table, exclusive terracotta for the garden, as well as an eclectic mix of European furniture and architectural antiques. It also offers custom sourcing and import services for one-of-a-kind, estate-sized terracotta objects. 440 Common St., Belmont, Massachusetts 02478 Tel. (866) 337-8821.

www.Sfoggio.com
www.DerutaImports.com
ww.GardenPlanters.com
www.DomesticTemple.com

Society for the Preservation of New England Antiquities (SPNEA), a regional organization headquartered in Boston, owns and operates 35 properties from the seventeenth century to the present. SPNEA shares New England's architecture, landscapes, objects, and people's stories through innovative programs for residents, visitors, and scholars from all over the world. One of its properties is Codman House in Lincoln, Massachusetts, at (781) 259-8843. SPNEA's address is 141 Cambridge St., Boston, Massachusetts 02114. Tel. (617) 227-3956.

SpiritMetals creations by Vassa have been commissioned by corporations and homeowners. Her objective is to create metal art that combines the strength and power of metal with the beauty and energy of nature. To obtain her soft and fluid shapes, she uses Mig and Arc welding along with her plasma cutter. 3384 Black Willow Trail, Deland, Florida 32724 Tel. (386) 943-3711.

www.spiritmetal.com *or* vassa@spiritmetal.com

Stone Forest, Inc., has been creating hand-carved granite sculptures, which combine the elegant simplicity of Japanese tradition with contemporary design since 1989. The integrity of granite gives Stone Forest carvings a radiant presence. The individual character of stone, as well as the inspiration of the stonecutter, lends to each sculpture a unique quality. 213 South St. Francis Dr., Santa Fe, New Mexico 87501 Tel. (505) 986-8883 .

www. Stoneforest.com
info@stoneforest.com

TJ's at the Sign of the Goose is a former farmhouse transformed into designer showrooms. The garden delights and surprises with its meandering paths, one-of-a-kind birdhouses, and unique plantings. Urns spill over with exotic foliage, statuary peeks out from abundant flowers, life-size animals hide among the greenery, and an amazing array of sundials clock the time. 1287 US Route 1, Cape Neddick, Maine 03902 Tel. (207) 363-5673 .

wwwtjsgoose.com
info@tjsgoose.com

Tom Torrens has produced quality designed, functional works of art for the home and garden for the past 30 years. Today, his designs can be found all over the world. His works include bells, gongs, fountains, birdbaths, bird feeders, sundials, gazing globes, garden gates, world globes, and custom doors. P.O. Box 1819, Gig Harbor, Washington 98335 Tel. (253) 857-5831.

www.tomtorrens.com
ttorrens@tomtorrens.com

Waterloo Gardens in Devon and Exton, Pennsylvania, is a Main Line gardening tradition. Waterloo boasts the area's largest selection of plants, landscaping design and building service, outdoor and indoor lighting, garden accessories, gifts, collectibles, and casual furniture. A visit to Waterloo Gardens is not another shopping trip; it's an experience. 200 N. Whitford Rd., Exton, Pennsylvania 19341 Tel. (610) 363-0800 and at 136 Lancaster Ave., Devon, Pennsylvania 19333 Tel. (610) 293-0800.

www.waterloogardens.com

Weston Nurseries of Hopkinton assists its clients in designing, creating, and enjoying outdoor living areas. Relying on environmentally sound practices, it produces quality plants and offers trees, shrubs, and perennials that produce the best results in this region. It has a wide range of garden accessories including pools and garden trains. Route 135, Hopkinton, Massachusetts Tel. (508) 435-3414.

www.westonnurseries.com
CustomerService@WestonNurseries.com

Chris Williams, artist and sculptor, began his career in 1994, designing and creating sculpture using found metal objects. Today, in addition to found objects, Chris works with steel and bronze for new and commissioned pieces. Each sculpture is one of a kind, welded and forged signifying his unique style. His Iron Works of Art are wildlife sculptures outside the box. 80 Grove St., Gloucester, Massachusetts 01930 Tel. (978) 281-7252.

Ironworks@Art.com

Ralph Williams is the man to call when you want to have a spectacular garden railway built in your backyard. He and his son, Eric Peterson, have become synonymous with creative landscaping ideas and have created some of the most impressive backyard railroads and pool designs anywhere. Ralph, Eric, and their team of dedicated workers have built more than 40 garden railways of all sizes in the New England area.

Willowbrook Garden at Spring Wood Gallery is a labor of love. Paul and Ann Breeden have designed peaceful, meandering paths that encircle imaginatively planted garden beds. The intricate lines of ornamental grasses and dwarf bamboo, the verdant mosses, and the blooms of elegant water lilies promise a display of ever-changing beauty. *Yankee Magazine* acclaimed this gallery of paintings, prints, and sculpture; it has been featured on HGTV. Route 200, Sullivan, Maine Tel. (207) 422-3007.

Yardbirds' Richard Kolb finds that making Yardbirds is more fun than work. Each Yardbird is unique, whimsical, funny, and guaranteed to bring pleasure. He uses mostly scrap and recycled parts to create his menagerie of metal birds, critters, dogs, and cats. It is pretty simple. Yardbirds are really just about happiness. 2921 South 2nd St., Louisville, Kentucky 40208 Tel. (502) 637-8752 or (800) 828-9247.

Nohra Yuille's container gardening allows our imaginations to play. Her containers can be seen as canvases on which she paints our pictures, whether they are an alpine scene or a moss green study. Nohra Yuille's moss gardens were featured in a special publication of *Better Homes and Gardens*. 46 Grove St., Essex, Connecticut 06426 Tel. (860) 767-3465.

Maintaining Your Garden Ornaments

Garden ornaments are magical when they are just dusted with snow or peaking out of a snowdrift. The downside of this beauty is that if we want to enjoy our garden ornaments throughout the year, they will age – just like we do.

True, some exposure improves ornaments. The mold or dirt that fills the cracks and crevices on a statue can add to its appeal, but in the long run minuscule cracks can lead to rust or cause the ornament to split apart. Wood does decay; cast iron does rust.

To protect all objects, place them on a pedestal of some sort, provide good air circulation, and divert sprinklers. Occasionally, remove the dirt and mold.

Marble's luster has attracted sculptors for centuries. Although some consider today's sculptors not as skilled as in the past, all marble statues are individually made. Water or stains can easily penetrate marble, which is extremely porous. To wash marble, use distilled water and a mild abrasive detergent that contains no bleach.

Limestone with its warm tones belongs in cool or misty areas. There, moss and lichens will quickly grow on it.

To maintain marble or limestone pieces, consider placing them in a protected area or gently rinsing them after each rainfall. Acid rain is corrosive.

Ice and wind can damage a statue. If a statue is not secure on its base, lower it early in the winter.

Before winter, gently remove excess dirt and insulate a statue from the cold by a weatherproof tarp. If water freezes in unsealed surface cracks, the piece can split.

Today's cast stone garden ornaments are generally cement based. They look like carved limestone or sandstone. Terra cotta ornaments are commonly used in the garden for pots.

Freezing and thawing can damage concrete and terra cotta containers. I was dismayed one winter to find that my birdbath had frozen and cracked. When water freezes, it expands and can crack concrete.

The birds need the water in the winter but look for a better container than your concrete birdbath. All water should be removed from fountains and birdbaths before the first frost. The birdbath bowl should be removed and placed upside down somewhere safe.

Waterproofing your concrete accessory is a good way to guard against cracking. Apply a one- time treatment of a silicon-based water seal or a thin layer of white cement, which bonds well to concrete surfaces. Or use paint formulated for outdoor use and reapply it annually. Where possible, turn over or cover birdbaths or pots to prevent them from collecting water.

Cast iron urns with drainage holes do not need protection. Those without holes should be tipped over or covered during the winter. To prevent rust-causing moisture on cast iron, apply an appropriate paint or paste wax before placing the object in the garden.

Terra cotta pots are porous, which allows the roots of the plants to breathe. Once those tiny pores fill with water and the temperature drops, those pores expand causing the clay pot to break. Whether the pots have a drainage hole or not, they should be brought inside or upended for the winter.

Fountains and basins deserve special attention. Drain the water from the plumbing to prevent costly freeze-ups. Pots, jars, and birdbaths should be positioned to prevent water from accumulating.

Generally, sundials are impervious to the winter. If they are in a windy location, you might wish to attach them permanently to their base.

The easiest solution is to bring the ornament inside. Most of us don't however.